The Shape of the World

Ovals

Dana Meachen Rau

Marshall Cavendish
Benchmark
New York

Ovals grow.

Ovals crack.

Ovals mix.

Ovals are cold.

Ovals are for races.

Ovals can be fruit.

Ovals can be bugs.

15

Ovals can be letters.

17

You can make an
oval!

19

Ovals

bugs

eggs

fruit

ice rink

letters

race track

seeds

spoon

21

Index

Page numbers in **boldface** are illustrations.

About the Author

Dana Meachen Rau is an author, editor, and illustrator. A graduate of Trinity College in Hartford, Connecticut, she has written more than one hundred fifty books for children, including nonfiction, biographies, early readers, and historical fiction. She lives with her family in Burlington, Connecticut.

Reading Consultants

Nanci Vargus, Ed.D. is an Assistant Professor of Elementary Education at the University of Indianapolis.

Beth Walker Gambro received her M.S. Ed. Reading from the University of St. Francis, Joliet, Illinois.

With thanks to Nanci Vargus, Ed.D. and
Beth Walker Gambro, reading consultants

Marshall Cavendish Benchmark
Marshall Cavendish
99 White Plains Road
Tarrytown, New York 10591-9001
www.marshallcavendish.us

Library of Congress Cataloging-in-Publication Data

Rau, Dana Meachen, 1971–
Ovals / by Dana Meachen Rau.
p. cm. — (Bookworms. The shape of the world)
Summary: "Identifies ovals in the world"—Provided by publisher.
Includes index.
ISBN-13: 978-0-7614-2281-5
ISBN-10: 0-7614-2281-1
1. Ovals—Juvenile literature. 2. Curves—Juvenile literature. 3. Geometry, Plane—Juvenile literature.
I. Title. II. Series.
QA483.R38 2006
516'.154—dc22
2005032456

Photo Research by Anne Burns Images

Cover Photo by Corbis/Alan Schein Photography

The photographs in this book are used with permission and through the courtesy of:
SuperStock: pp. 1, 9, 13L, 20BLL, 20BR age fotostock; p. 7 BananaStock; pp. 13R, 20BLR Food Collection.
Corbis: pp. 3, 15R, 20TLR, 21BL Royalty Free; pp. 5, 20TR Elmar Krenkel/zefa; pp. 11, 21TR Sam Sharpe;
pp. 15L, 20TLL Robert Llewellyn; p. 19 Tom & Dee Ann McCarthy; p. 21BR Sagel & Kranefeld/zefa.

Printed in Malaysia
1   3   5   6   4   2